GOYA

GOYA

INTRODUCTION BY

ENRIQUE LAFUENTE FERRARI

8 . III . 86

A MENTOR-UNESCO ART BOOK

PUBLISHED BY
THE NEW AMERICAN LIBRARY, NEW YORK AND TORONTO
BY ARRANGEMENT WITH UNESCO

FIRST PRINTING, NOVEMBER, 1966

MENTOR TRADEMARK REG. U. S. PAT. OFF. AND FOREIGN COUNTRIES
REGISTERED TRADEMARK—MARCA REGISTRADA

MENTOR-UNESCO ART BOOKS ARE PUBLISHED IN THE UNITED STATES BY
THE NEW AMERICAN LIBRARY, INC.,
1301 AVENUE OF THE AMERICAS, NEW YORK, NEW YORK 10019,
IN CANADA BY THE NEW AMERICAN LIBRARY OF CANADA LIMITED,
295 KING STREET EAST, TORONTO 2, ONTARIO
PRINTED IN ITALY BY AMILCARE PIZZI S.P.A. MILANO

The first biographical details we have about Goya were printed in one of the earliest catalogues (1828) of the museum now called the Prado, then known as the Galería del Museo del Rey. Opposite the first of Goya's works to be shown in the Museum, an equestrian portrait of Queen María Luisa, appeared this brief and succinct entry: " Francisco Goya. Born at Fuendetodos, Aragon, in 1746. Nominated Painter to the King in 1786 and later made Senior Court Painter; now on a pension for old age. He was a pupil of Don José Luzán in Saragossa, who taught him the principles of draughtsmanship by making him copy his best engravings. He spent four years with him, and then began to paint with originality until he went to Rome. He had no other master than his own observation of famous paintings and painters in Rome and Spain, from which he drew greatest profit." This simple note gains great value by the editor's footnote: "Article communicated by himself"; that is, the note was written by Goya. In his own words, Goya shows himself to be the first great self-taught artist in modern painting; and it might well be said that what we call modern art today has, to a great extent, been carried out by self-taught painters. Those who, like Berenson, have little sympathy for modern art have condemned Goya as its precursor. " With him ", said the great American critic, " modern anarchy began."

The eighteenth century saw the beginning of the great European crisis in art, science and politics—of the desire to replace the old social order by a more just and rational society. There was also a sharp rise in secularization, which had started under the Renaissance but had declined with religious discord and the rise of absolute monarchies. According to Weisbach, baroque art had lost the sacred and enlightening inspiration it knew in the seventeenth century. Its high ideals were lost in the frivolity of rococo. Philosophy and scepticism had undermined the deep-rooted convictions and beliefs which had given substance to Western culture ever since the Middle Ages. Art, through its link with reality, was bound to express this critical situation. And it was to be Goya, a spontaneous and self-taught painter born in a country on the fringe of Europe, isolated since the time of Philip II from social and cultural reform—Goya, who carried out the tremendous task of striking new roads in painting. The road leading to a new social and cultural structure lay in freedom from routine and prejudice; in a word, it was liberty. André Malraux, speaking of Goya more sympathetically than Berenson, said that " he prefigures all modern art, for modern art was born of this freedom ".

This is even more surprising as Goya's painting went against the currents of his time. There is an obvious *décalage* between thought and painting in eighteenth-century Europe. The return to classical antiquity, which dominated political thought, literature and the arts in the second half of that century, tried to impose its fanatical dogmas on painting as well: a noble art composed of rigid discipline, inspired by classical statues and the archaeological excavations of Pompeii and Herculaneum. All art inspired by reality and life was rejected as vulgar. An intellectual art was dominant, and found expression in what we call neo-classicism. This originated with Mengs, painter to the King of Spain, whom Goya knew in Madrid, and reached its height with Jacques Louis David, who in pre-revolutionary France painted dramatic scenes of the Roman Republic with the evident intention of moralizing. An academic in the strictest sense of the word, David, dictator of the arts under the Revolution and the Empire, initiated what we call *pompier* art. Goya was, strictly speaking, a contemporary of David and the neo-classical generation, but his art, through its sheer impulse and undeniable genius, was diametrically opposed to their aesthetic direction. Though admired by his contemporaries, Goya often disconcerted them by the bold freedom of his paintings: it is only now that the advanced genius of his art has been understood. If the work of a genius is the expression of his time, it is often, as Ortega y Gasset pointed out, in opposition to the dominant currents of his time.

Goya was born at Fuendetodos, a very poor village in Aragon, on 30 March 1746. Philip V, the first Bourbon monarch, was on the throne of Spain and Louis XV, his nephew, reigned over France. Goya's father was a gilder in Saragossa, the capital of Aragon, and it was there that Goya spent his childhood and adolescence. Only a few local painters kept up a languid artistic life in the city. José Luzán was a baroque painter who had studied at Naples. Goya went to him to learn draughtsmanship, but as he himself said, learned very little. With the awakening of his originality, which made him restless and rebellious to academic discipline, Goya thought of trying his luck elsewhere. He went to Madrid where the Bourbons had set up the Real Academia de Bellas Artes which gave scholarships to young artists. There he took part in painting competitions in 1763 and 1766, but failed in both. In an age when academic severity was predominant, self-tuition was no great aid to the young artist's chances of success. The ideal of all artists at that time was a scholarship enabling them to study in Rome. Since Goya could not win this, he decided to go to Italy at his own expense.

Goya's development as a painter was very different from that of the " old masters "; it more resembled the careers of great modern artists. It has been said that his development was intermittent, but this is merely an attempt to rationalize the astounding and unforeseeable variations of his art, which came in sudden spurts of energy rising from the very depths of his creative genius rather than from outside influences or the organic development of his own talents. These outbursts were linked to events in his life, and occurred abruptly at given moments, as a reaction to new internal or external situations. These are what we have called Goya's " crises ".

All the different schools of painting between his century and ours seem to have been foreshadowed by Goya himself. He was at first an ardent follower of the baroque style. However, if his early religious paintings were in the baroque tradition, he later put himself " in tune " with his century, by adopting the frivolities of the *ancien régime* on the eve of the French Revolution. The opening of this era was also a milestone in his own life: on 25 July 1773, in Madrid, Goya married Josefa Bayeu, whose brother was Francisco Bayeu, one of the leading painters in Saragossa. Francisco Bayeu had worked for ten years in Madrid with Mengs, the Bohemian artist called to Charles III's court to supervise his artistic undertakings. Bayeu obtained work for his brother-in-law and protégé in the Royal Tapestry Factory, a court dependency which recruited young artists to supply it with cartoons. These tapestry cartoons represent an extremely important part of Goya's training in the use of colours. They drew him away from the religious genre, for which he had no feeling. They enriched his composition and satisfied his vocation as an observer of life, teaching him to give his figures motion and to apply his bold brushwork to humanist themes which were rare in academic painting. Goya, who was a commoner, now had the opportunity to paint a wide range of ordinary people in their pastimes, amusements and daily tasks. Popular life was the subject of these tapestries woven for the adornment of royal palaces and reflecting the philanthropy which the eighteenth century had brought into vogue.

Goya's work between 1774 and 1792 was intermittent but fruitful. Painting tapestry cartoons eased his hand in a genre which allowed him great freedom, and which, as they were manufactured industrially, did not overwhelm him with responsibility. At last he had found what his temperament craved: liberty. He produced more than fifty cartoons. Stacked up in the factory as used models, they remained in oblivion until the 1868 revolution, when almost all were found and taken to the Prado where today they give us the lightest and happiest introduction to Goya. Here we can but mention some of the most brilliant among them, which soon made Goya famous. His son tells us that while he was under Mengs' supervision the Bohemian artist was astounded by his fluency, spontaneity and magnificent use of colours.

The Parasol, finished in 1777, was the culmination of less than three years of work on tapestry cartoons. A lively play of yellows, blues and greens contrasts with the warm red and brown tones of earlier pictures. Goya was already Goya, but at this stage his painting expressed the *joie de vivre* of a world still optimistic in that golden autumn of the *ancien régime*. In *The Pottery Seller*, another masterpiece delivered to the Tapestry Factory in 1779, refinement goes yet further and the composition is more complex; in Goya's world the aristocracy and the people live side by side; he is more self-confident and his painting has conquered the expression of movement.

He fell seriously ill in 1778, and during his convalescence started working on etchings and aquatints. His first attempts were unexceptional, but they gave him the opportunity of studying the works of Velázquez, from whom he learned the essential lessons for his future work as a portraitist. By 1780 he had already achieved some small measure of fame as a painter in Madrid; he was elected member of the Real Academia de Bellas Artes, and though the Christ he painted for this occasion is a cold and lifeless picture, in this same year he finished some new tapestry cartoons among which we find a particularly beautiful work, *The Washerwomen*. In 1780 also, Goya publicly showed for the first time his nonconformity with academic painting of the time. While painting some frescoes for the church of Our Lady of Pilar in Saragossa, Francisco Bayeu, Goya's brother-in-law, reproved him for what he termed his frivolity: for a pupil of Mengs, his work was careless and faulty. Goya, already conscious of his talent and of his opposition to the aesthetic discipline to which he was expected to submit, took umbrage at these remarks and severed all relations with Bayeu. He then tried to shake off this humiliation and break out of the narrow confines of tapestry design. But attempts at cultivating the normal style of the time brought him small success, and the quick triumph he longed for still eluded him. His portrait of *The Count of Florida-blanca* (1783) and his altarpiece *The Sermon of Saint Bernardino of Siena*, for the church of Saint Francis of Madrid (1784), were concessions to the current style, as were other religious paintings in which he either followed his baroque initiation or tried, unsuccessfully, to imitate Mengs. This was not his style. He found it in one of the themes of great painters of all times: portraiture. For Goya the portrait was, above all, a problem of the technique of painting; but, as with Velázquez and Rembrandt, the passionate search for the mystery of the human individual was never absent. The most important thing for him was to go straight to the heart, to sum up quickly his model's character. His son wrote, many years after his death, that the portraits which had given the artist greatest satisfaction were those of his friends, for which he needed not more than one sitting. Spontaneity, rapidity, frank and gay execution were Goya's ideals in portrait painting. He was always affected by his models, and so his portraits could be very unequal. His liking or revulsion for the person before him were unmistakably reflected in his painting. Beauty, goodness, intelligence, gentility, timidity, vanity, pride, stupidity, can all be seen in Goya's work, sometimes portrayed with surprising sincerity. He neither described nor analysed, made no attempts at psychology; his insight into character was undeniably intuitive, but lacked the impassiveness of Velázquez who was lordly but generous. For Goya was of the people and loved and hated without control.

Passionately fond of women, it was women who led him to the pinnacle of success and who furnished him with subjects for his masterpieces. Madrid society was then under the sway of women: at court there was Crown Princess María Luisa of Bourbon-Parma, a disciple of Condillac, elegant, coquettish, frivolous; among the aristocracy, brilliant women like the Duchesses of Osuna and Alba. They befriended Goya and gave him access to the most exclusive Madrid society, without making him forgo his old interests: hunting, popular dancing, bullfights....

It was about 1785 when Goya began to move in high society. His first benefactress was the Duchess of Osuna, who was not very pretty but intelligent and vivacious. He painted her and her husband and decorated their country house with exquisite paintings in which he took full advantage of his experience as a tapestry designer. Among the paintings for the Osuna house was *Saint Isidore's Meadow*, which had perhaps been intended as another tapestry. It shows the refined economy of palette and brushwork that Goya had achieved. In this painting the festivals in which all social classes mingled in the Madrid of Charles III were vivaciously portrayed against the silvery background of the court buildings on the banks of the Manzanares; the crowd was interpreted by means of minute and expressive brush-strokes, as an Impressionist might have done. About 1786, he painted the admirable portrait of *The Marchioness of Pontejos*, now in the National Gallery of Washington, one of the most exquisite female portraits in the whole of the eighteenth century, and finely orchestrated in those greys for which Goya became famous. At that period Goya also painted Charles III, an indefatigable hunter, probably without having the monarch pose for him; Goya backed the figure with wide stretches of landscape, in the manner of Velázquez whom he had always admired. He also painted the most important financiers of the budding Spanish bourgeoisie. These portraits now hang in the Banco de España. The best among them is the portrait of *The Count of Cabarrús* (1788), a French merchant settled in Madrid, father of the famous Madame Tallien. Goya was already forty when in 1786 he was nominated Painter to the King; his beginnings had not been easy, but from then to 1808 his social career was marked with success.

New heights awaited Goya on the death of the old and virtuous king, Charles III. Charles IV and María Luisa quickly nominated him Senior Court Painter (1789). It was then that he painted the group of *The Duke of Osuna and his Family*. His technique is smooth and transparent, full of charm and elegance. The scarlet highlights of the

Duke's uniform admirably offset the range of greens and greys, and add to the charm of his wife's and children's faces. Goya painted the royal family often. The best of these paintings are the corpulent Charles IV in hunting dress, and the elegant but already wrinkled María Luisa in court dress, in the Royal Palace of Madrid. He was still painting his last tapestry cartoons at the time; the best of these are *Blind Man's Buff* (1789) and *The Country Wedding* (1791).

During this period of social recognition and success Goya met the leading Spanish writers and thinkers of the time. This is important, for these intellectual groups in a country which, during the eighteenth century, had tried to assimilate modern ideas and to correct the errors of its past history, were in the direct line of European culture in the century of Enlightenment and the Encyclopaedia. They were progressive and liberal; their criticism of the society in which they lived and their desire for much needed reform influenced Goya and coincided with his own feelings. To understand certain aspects of his genius we must realize that he, exceptionally, was not indifferent to the situation of the people. Like so many Spaniards of his time, in those years when Europe was bubbling over with ideas of revolution, Goya sympathized with liberty and condemned the abuses of an archaic social structure.

At the very height of his success Goya passed through a terrible crisis. In the autumn of 1792 he was travelling to Andalucia, perhaps to paint part of a chapel in Cadiz, when he was struck down by a violent illness in Seville. Several medical writers have tried, with far-fetched hypotheses, to make a retrospective diagnosis. Some have mentioned cerebral syphilis, and others thrombosis; Jovellanos called it apoplexy. The fact remains, however, that for some time he could not paint. His convalescence was long and ended (like Beethoven's, though for other reasons) in total deafness. For many long months his career seemed to be in danger. Yet the tremendous energy and vitality of the artist, which he retained into old age, pulled him through. But to an extravert like Goya, who enjoyed life to the full, this accident in the midst of success was a severe crisis. His art was transformed; a different Goya was born.

This frank, jovial man, who loved society, conversation, theatres, bullfights and his friends, was now cut off from it all by deafness, isolated from dealings with his fellow men by the solitude of silence. This cruel blow turned him into an introvert, a pessimist. But his painting did not suffer by it; in fact, with his illness there developed a bitter power for forms which spilled over in drawings and etchings. Goya, who had begun by engraving paintings after Velázquez, was to become one of the leading graphic artists of all time.

It is not only in his engravings that we see the impact of the crisis but also in a new type of painting: imaginative pictures in which he gives full expression to his interior world. His ideas are given forms. His technique becomes more free and daring, and his palette more violent and personal. When Goya fully recovered the use of his palette and paint-brushes it was to start on these imaginative pictures. A valuable testimony of this can be found in a letter he sent to a friend, the writer, diplomat and academician Don Bernardo de Iriarte on 4 February 1794. It was a confession of his renewed desire for freedom in painting: " To occupy my imagination so sorely tried by my illness ... I have dedicated myself to painting a series of cabinet pictures to which I have added my own comments. This is impossible in the case of commissioned paintings where caprice and inventiveness have no scope for development." Let us underline the words *imagination*, *caprice* and *development*, for they define the new spirit of Goya's art after the crisis of his illness, the desire that his painting should break the bonds by which the artist considered himself bound in his commissioned work; in brief, these words show his craving for liberty and creativeness. The new Goya decided to be himself, and this is what the word *development* implies. From now on his painting would be untrammelled, and he would paint as the spirit moved him. Influenced by his new attitude to the world, a new kind of painting germinated freely. It was in advance of its time and knew no limits or precedent to its daring. Goya felt suffocated by the discipline imposed on art in his time and, sure of himself, he shed all those academic prejudices which had restrained, albeit lightly, the overflowing of his talent. The pictures he sent to Don Bernardo de Iriarte were, he said, " popular diversions ", but among them was *The Mad House*, which by no stretch of the imagination could be called a popular diversion. As we do not know exactly which pictures date from 1794, we must relate to Goya's new frame of mind paintings such as those in the Academia de Bellas Artes in Madrid, whatever their date, for they would in any case have been painted after his illness. Among the pictures at the Academia are some which may be considered as diversions or popular festivals such as *The Burial of the Sardine*, a carnival scene, and *The Bullfight* in a village. His critical view of traditional Spain appears in *The Tribunal of the Inquisition* and in *The Procession of Flagellants*. Goya, influenced by the ideas of his age, in touch with intellectual Spanish circles which sought a reform of traditional Spain, denounced intolerance and superstition, and aspired to a more rational world.

Goya remained totally deaf; it was said in 1794 that the only way to communicate with him was by writing. But he did not lose his sensitivity to humanity and beauty, as we see in some exquisite portraits done in the famous Goya grey, like *The Marchioness of Pontejos*. It was probably at this time that he painted *Doña Tadea Arias de Enríquez*, a symphony of greys and blacks in perfect harmony with the young woman's beauty. It was about 1794 too that he embarked upon a relationship with the Duchess of Alba whose elegance and strength of character impressed him to the point of falling in love, platonically or otherwise. He painted her in 1795, vivacious, intelligent and domineering, in a portrait whose greys sing softly in tune with the brilliant red of the sash and laces. In 1796 he also painted her husband and cousin *The Duke of Alba*, Marquis of Villafranca, a melancholic character in poor health who had not much longer to live. Goya took great pains over this portrait of the duke as a music lover, with one of Haydn's sonatas in his hand. The meticulous lines and delicate tones seem to adapt themselves to the aristocratic mode. A year later, the duke died and Goya accompanied the duchess on a trip to her estates in Andalucia. It was there that he painted the beautiful portrait of the lady dressed in grey, now in the Hispanic Society of America. We are also reminded of the duchess in the miniature portrait called *The Flirtation*, in which a lady dressed in black receives the homage of an attentive courtier.

In Sanlúcar, surrounded by the duchess and her little court, the deaf painter began work on the preliminary sketches which were to become his series of etchings, *The Caprices*. Gradually Goya's original idea developed into a condemnation of sinful humanity, dragged along by its vices and passions. In these etchings no state, profession or social class was free from his stinging sarcasm: nobles, legal practitioners, doctors, prostitutes, monks, witches, procuresses appear as a cross-section of incorrigible and degraded humanity. Together with this social criticism there appears in his art the world of the subconscious: "The dream of reason produces monsters", he declared at the foot of one of his etchings, and in seeking a graphic language to express this abysmal world, Goya, a true precursor of modern art, freely distorted his figures. The whole venture was daring. When he published *The Caprices* in 1799 he had to withdraw them from sale for fear of being indicted by the Inquisition which was again becoming a force in face of the menace of the French Revolution. We should not forget that Goya's crisis coincided with the Reign of Terror in France, and that through his intellectual friends and the gazettes of the time the artist was made aware of the commotion that was shaking Europe, contradictory echoes of which were reaching Spain. Portraits of his political and literary friends poured out: *Meléndez Valdés*, the poet (1797), *Don Bernardo de Iriarte* (1797), *Moratín* (1799), *Jovellanos* (1798), the great patrician who for a few months was a minister under Charles IV. His illustrious friend's brief passage in power gave Goya the opportunity to paint one

15

of the works most typical of his change of style and of his new freedom of technique: the frescoes in the church of San Antonio de la Florida. In this monumental painting we see his pitiless and sarcastic vision and his rich and varied portrayal of humanity. Using a religious theme as a pretext—a miracle of Saint Anthony of Padua—Goya exhibits his repertory of human beings grouped in the dome, among whom we see credulity, indifference, vanity and misery. Charming women beside monstrous procuresses, devotees, beggars, tramps, lovers, children, make the frescoes in this small church for palace servants into a colossal cartoon, expressionist and superlatively free. A few years ago the author of this book discovered and published a splendid sketch for the dome of La Florida, now in the Pittsburgh Museum.

After *The Caprices* and frescoes, Goya's portraits became smoother and bolder, even when he painted the royal family, his main occupation during those years. *Queen María Luisa in a Mantilla*, painted at the Granja in the summer of 1799, showed that the great colourist, with blacks, pinks and greys, could make an admirable likeness full of character. In the Escorial that same year he painted the equestrian portraits of Charles IV and the queen, and in 1800 at Aranjuez he started on the sketches for the picture of *The Family of Charles IV*, a masterpiece of court portraiture which, for richness of colour, penetrating assessment of character and technical boldness, has few rivals. Remembering *Las Meninas* (The Noble Maidens) by Velázquez, Goya included himself in the picture as a shadowy figure in the background. The undoubted masterpiece of this period was the portrait of *The Countess of Chinchón*, Doña Maria Teresa of Bourbon, daughter of the Infante Don Luis, the younger son of Charles III, who had been banished from court for having contracted a morganatic marriage. This, with *The Marchioness of Pontejos*, is the gem among Goya's feminine portraits.

Court favour brought Goya the nomination as Senior Court Painter in October 1799. He painted a ceremonial portrait of Godoy glorifying him as the victor in the ephemeral war declared against Portugal in 1801 to please

Napoleon. This series of masterly portraits continued with *The Count of Fernán Núñez* (1803), *The Marquis San Adrián* (1804), the painter's son *Xavier Goya*, *The Marchioness of Santa Cruz*, *Doña Isabel Cobos de Porcel* (about 1806), *Doña Antonia Zárate*, *Doña Sabasa García* and the full-length portrait of the actress Maria del Rosario Fernández, *La Tirana*. The two Majas, those paintings about which so much has been written, are believed to have been painted at that time. Though the actual date has been much discussed, it must have been earlier than 1808. Both paintings show the same woman, nude in one and wearing the popular dress of a Maja in the other. The two portraits are the same size, which has led to the belief that, as in other similar cases, they were meant for a private collection where the image of the clothed woman covered the nude and, by some contrivance, could uncover it at will. In few other cases can we see so well the flexibility of Goya's talent as in these two paintings, finished in the same period. *The Maja Nude* shows careful fine brushwork and cold tones, while *The Maja Clothed* has been painted with a warm palette, bold brushwork, smooth and almost Impressionist execution. We only know that these pictures were in the collection of the minister Godoy on his fall from power in 1808.

Goya was approaching a new crisis, which this time was simultaneous with an historical crisis. Napoleon secretly decided to carry out his policy of converting all European countries into feudal units of his empire, and to dethrone the Bourbons in Spain to give the throne to a member of his family. The court at Madrid furthered Bonaparte's designs through its thoughtlessness and intrigues. But Napoleon repaid their support by fostering a popular uprising which on 19 March 1808 forced Charles IV to abdicate in favour of the heir apparent, who then became Ferdinand VII. As Godoy was deposed and imprisoned, the abdication was popular. The new king created hopes which he was not to fulfil. Napoleon made as if to protect Godoy and the royal family, calling them to France. But it was all a trick. In the end all the Spanish Bourbons, including the new king, were in Bayonne. The country was alarmed, and on 2 May 1808 the people attacked French troops. Repression was brutal ... patriots fell before execution squads. But now the uprising spread to all the Spanish provinces. The government was disorganized, the army thrown into disarray, the citizens divided, and the war of resistance against the French took on at the same time the character of civil war. Disgusted with the ineptitude and immorality of the last reign, some illustrious Spaniards saw in French intervention the possibility of a beneficial reform for Spain. Others, like the majority of the Spanish people, decided to fight at all costs against foreign domination. A guerrilla war started, followed by repression. From 1808 to 1814 Spain was torn apart and bleeding from the wounds inflicted by the War of Independence, which the English, now allied to the Spanish insurrection, called the Peninsular War. Meanwhile, the Bourbons abdicated and Joseph Bonaparte became King of Spain.

All these events influenced the life and work of Goya. He had overcome the difficulties caused by his illness and deafness. His art was rejuvenated, and he himself was at the zenith of his career. But now the world was collapsing around him. War was a new and dramatic phase. His friends, most of them illustrious men, were divided; some were pro-French, ready to collaborate with Joseph Bonaparte, while others believed that national dignity could not tolerate Spain being overrun by Napoleon's troops. Goya stayed in Madrid for a while and then left for Saragossa, which was defending itself against the French. Here he painted a number of war scenes. Then Madrid surrendered, and Goya had his title of Court Painter confirmed by the new king, Joseph. These were dark years when, at times, the only centre of resistance was the impregnable city of Cadiz, where the Spaniards, helped by the English, brought about a political revolution and, in the name of Ferdinand VII, gave themselves a liberal constitution.

They were dark years for Goya as well, as he witnessed disaster after disaster, with blood flowing and passions unleashed. His life as a professional painter was limited—

a few commissions, a few portraits. Among his best works of this time must be counted the portrait of *Canon Llorente*, " the Spanish Voltaire ". But his appetite for creation did not die; he painted scenes of war in miniature which he kept in his home, and imaginative pictures painted with greater ease and liberty.

His pessimism became deeper. When the allied troops entered Madrid, he painted General Wellington. Man seemed to him nothing more than a bloodthirsty animal; his dreams of liberty and rationality were overshadowed. At the same time he continued his passionate condemnation of man in his brilliant series *The Disasters of War*, a collection of eighty-two etchings in which he gives us his personal view of the war. *The Disasters of War* are not a glorification of a national struggle; there are no heroes or villains. It is man he accuses in these impressive scenes of executions, burnings, siege, rape and ambush. It is the four horsemen of the Apocalypse galloping over a battered country. War is not exalted here; in these etchings he depicts hunger and suffering, devastation, horror and barbaric cruelty. There is no document in the history of art more terrifying and more accusatory than Goya's *Disasters of War*.

In the end, however, he had to keep his etchings without publishing them, for the last ones refer not to the war itself but to the post-war period, which brought to Goya, as it so often does, a new crop of sorrows and lost illusions.

Napoleon's luck ran out in the countries at the two ends of Europe—Spain and Russia. Ferdinand VII returned to the throne of Spain, but instead of trying to heal her wounds through peace he set about persecuting the liberal patriots. Those who were pro-French emigrated to escape execution, and the progressives were imprisoned. As a result, Goya found himself without friends. His solitude and pessimism grew, but he did not give up his art: he still had so much to say. It was after the end of the war, in 1814, before Ferdinand VII's entry into Madrid, that he painted the two great pictures today in the Prado: *The Second of May 1808 at the Puerta del Sol* and *The*

Firing Squad (*The Third of May 1808*), the two events which precipitated the War of Independence. Here again are two war paintings without rhetoric and without heroes.

Goya, though he was still court painter, did not enjoy the favour of Ferdinand VII. The king was painted by his favourite, Vicente López, who continued in the nineteenth century the old meticulous court-painter tradition and whose decorative work was borrowed directly from Mengs and the academic art of the eighteenth century. However, Goya received commissions from various official corporations and did several portraits of the king, undoubtedly without having the monarch pose for him. The most important are the two now in the Prado; in one of them Ferdinand VII, never a renowned military man (during his captivity in France as a guest of Talleyrand at the Chateau de Valençay he spent his time at the manly task of embroidery), was shown in the uniform of a general against the background of a military camp. The rich colours of the painting are backed by sure and confident execution, and the half-smile which the artist has grudgingly given the king creates an effect not far from caricature. If we compare Goya's portraits of Ferdinand VII with his delicate and sensitive paintings of *The Duke of Alba*, *The Maja Nude* or *The Countess of Chinchón*, we realize that here we are not so much following his development as an artist as observing his reactions, subconscious or otherwise, to his models. Ferdinand VII, a weak character, a vengeful son, a distrustful king, afraid of the dangers he had not faced during the war, was not an attractive model for Goya. The antipathy was mutual.

Goya had become a widower during the war, in 1812. He did not go to live with his son, who was already married, but with a woman, Leocadia Zorrilla, the wife of a certain Guillermo Weiss, who was the son of a German merchant settled in Madrid and who had left her in 1811 " because of her ill behaviour ". Apparently Doña Leocadia was related to the mother-in-law of Goya's son; he lived with her until he died. In 1814 in Madrid Doña Leocadia gave birth to a daughter, Rosario Weiss, who became a painter; though she took the name of her mother's husband, contemporaries considered her as Goya's daughter, and the old artist wanted her as a daughter, according to his own words. He was sixty-eight when Rosario was born; we can see that he was still vigorous in the admirable self-portrait signed and dated in 1815, now in the Academia de Bellas Artes. With its dark colours and masterly execution this reminds us of some of Rembrandt's self-portraits.

His vigour is also proved by some of the paintings of that time. He continued portraying the Madrid aristocracy who, in spite of the fact that the king no longer employed him, did not withdraw their favour. The portraits of *The Duke of San Carlos* (1815), *The Duchess of Abrantes* (1816), *The Duke of Osuna* in the Bonnat Museum, Bayonne, and the Secretary of the Academy, *Munárriz* (1815), show that his painting was taking the turn the Impressionists were soon to follow. An exceptional picture, representative of the new middle-class society which was to be increasingly important in the nineteenth century, is of the *Board of the Philippines Company*, in the Castres Museum. He carried on with his etchings, making a series of thirty-three in all, which he published in 1816 under the title of *Tauromachy*: lively impressions of bullfighting and its history, full of light and movement. In 1817 he went to Seville where the canon of the cathedral commissioned from him a picture of the holy martyrs Justa and Rufina. Murillo had treated the same subject and a comparison of the two pictures shows how the temperaments of the two artists differ. Goya also carried on painting his imaginative pictures for his own pleasure, large paintings, and also miniatures for which he sometimes worked on metal. Perhaps the masterpiece among them is *The Forge* in the Frick Collection in New York. Physical labour had always interested Goya (peace and toil are the central idea of the last page of the *Disasters—This is the Truth*—summarizing his impressions of the madness of war). But his characters are no longer the gaily dressed workers of the tapestry cartoons; they are rugged artisans of the nineteenth century. The tension and vitality of their movements are admirably captured in this painting. Here Goya limits his palette to black-tinged yellows, greys and dusky whites with one bright tone—the vivid streak of red-hot iron on the anvil.

His curiosity showed no signs of disappearing. He started learning lithography, and signed his first lithograph in 1819. That year he bought a house in the suburbs of Madrid, on the banks of the Manzanares, to isolate himself in the country for his last years beside his orchards and wells. Here he painted his best religious painting, in the same sombre tones that characterized that period: *The Last Communion of Saint Joseph Calasantius*.

Illness endangered his life again. An even more pessimistic Goya appeared after his recovery in 1820, in the so-called black paintings and the etchings of *The Incongruities* or *Proverbs*. A new crisis and a new style, an extension of what he had begun in *The Caprices* and in San Antonio de la Florida. An expressionist art, violent, painted in greyish ochre and black, covered the walls of his country house. Twisted imagination, hallucinations, supernatural visions were painted with greater spontaneity and sincerity than the sophisticated and photographic surrealism of our times. In one of these paintings he gives a maniacal interpretation of *The Pilgrimage of Saint Isidore*, which had been the subject of a charming little picture at the end of the eighteenth century. Monstrous, bloated witches, procuresses dragged down to the final degradation of decrepitude, hallucinated beggars are part of the strange procession marching with infernal deliberation. And can we not see a symbol of crazed humanity, devouring itself in the bloody flesh of its children, in the paranoic *Saturn* which decorates Goya's dining-room? The same enigmatic visionary temper is evident in *The Proverbs*, a series of etchings which he never completed and which remained unpublished for many years after his death.

The broken rhythm of Goya's life resembled the history of his country, which received another blow during his last years. Political reaction to Ferdinand VII provoked a military uprising in 1820 to re-establish the 1812 constitution; the king, afraid of revolution, hypocritically gave in. The chaotic situation which resulted was brought to an end three years later by foreign intervention. Goya undoubtedly watched the liberal movement with sympathy. When the army of the hundred thousand children of Saint Louis, executor of the agreements of the Holy Alliance, confirmed Ferdinand VII as absolute monarch, a new uprising took place, followed by further persecution and emigration of liberals. Goya must also have been afraid. Hidden in the house of a friend, an Aragonese priest, it was no doubt there that he painted Ramón Satué, a magistrate, the nephew of his host (1823).

Doña Leocadia's son, a liberal, had to emigrate to France. His mother wanted to follow him. Thus Goya, at the age of seventy-seven, decided to leave Spain as well. As Court Painter he had to ask for permission, justifying it on the pretext of taking the waters at Plombières in Burgundy. We do not know if he actually did so, but he went through Bordeaux to Paris, and on his return settled in Bordeaux near his pro-French friends and relatives who had emigrated in 1814. He liked the city and everything interested him.

He fell seriously ill in 1825, but recovered and in 1826 travelled to Spain to ask for a pension. At the age of eighty he still had the energy to travel over the back-breaking road to Madrid. His stay at court was brief, and he was soon back in Bordeaux, where he painted portraits of his friends and scenes of bullfights, and sketched unendingly. His last dated portraits were of *Jacques Galos*, the banker *Don Juan Bautista Muguiro*— " un Manet avant la lettre "— and *Don José Pio de Molina* which could almost be a Cézanne. His last homage to women, his constant source of inspiration, was *The Milkmaid of Bordeaux*. In the meantime he had painted miniatures, and the epic and barbaric scenes of bullfighting in Bordeaux in four great lithographs which can be counted among the masterpieces of this genre. Until the

23

end of his life he sought in art an unobstructed expression of his imagination, a rare gift among painters, seeking the development of his capacities and the free expansion of what he called his caprice. He died in Bordeaux on the night of 15 April 1828. A contemporary of Napoleon and Beethoven, Goya left a lasting impression on painting. He had carried out his own private revolution. It was a long time before his message was understood.

ILLUSTRATIONS

4

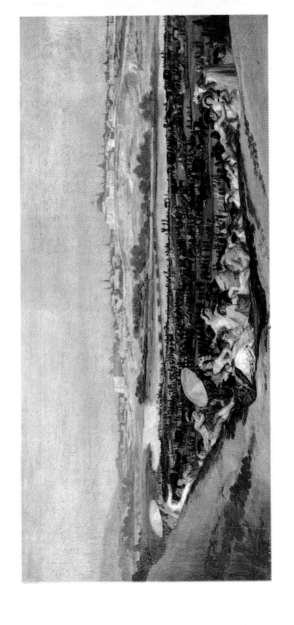

8

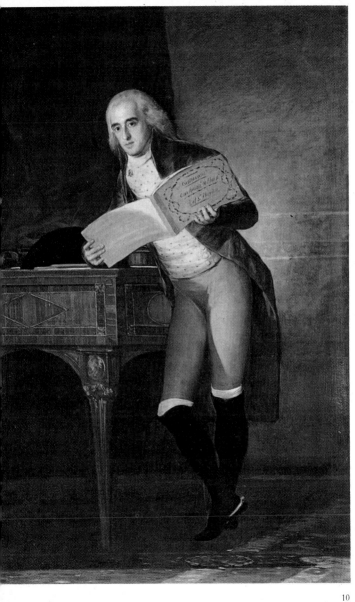

22

23

CONTENTS

The illustration reproduced on the back of the cover is a detail from Duel with Cudgels *(wall-painting transferred to canvas. 123 x 266 cm. Museo del Prado, Madrid.)*

With the exception of Plate 27, the colour photographs for this volume were specially taken by Mario Carrieri.

Continued overleaf ▶

ACKNOWLEDGMENTS

It is desired to thank all who gave assistance to the Unesco mission which visited Spain to collect material for this volume, in particular: the Spanish National Commission for Unesco; the Director and staff of the Museo Nacional del Prado, Madrid; the Director and staff of the Real Academia de Bellas Artes de San Fernando, Madrid; the Duke of Alba; the Duke of Sueca; the Duchess of Fernán Núñez; the Marchioness of La Romana.

BIBLIOGRAPHY

BERUETE, Aureliano de, *Goya as portrait painter*, translated by Selwyn Brinton, London, Constable, 1922.

BERUETE, Aureliano de, *Goya, composiciones y figuras*, Madrid, Blass, 1917.

BERUETE, Aureliano de, *Goya grabador*, Madrid, Blass, 1918.

CAMÓN, José, *Los Disparates y sus dibujos preparatorios*, Barcelona, Instituto Amatller de Arte Hispánico, 1950.

LAFUENTE FERRARI, Enrique, *La situación y la estela del arte de Goya*, preliminary study in the illustrated catalogue of the exhibition *Antecedentes, coincidencias e influencias del arte de Goya* organized by the Sociedad Española de Amigos del Arte, Madrid, 1947.

LAFUENTE FERRARI, Enrique, *Goya: the frescoes in San Antonio de la Florida in Madrid*, Geneva, Skira, 1955.

LAFUENTE FERRARI, Enrique, *La Tauromaquia*, Paris, Club français du livre, 1963.

MALRAUX, André, *Saturn: an essay on Goya*, translated by C. W. Chilton, New York, Phaidon, 1957.

MATHERON, Laurent, *Goya*, Paris, Schulz & Thuillié, 1858.

MAYER, August L., *Francisco de Goya*, translated by Robert West, London, Dent, 1924.

SÁNCHEZ CANTÓN, F. J., *Los Caprichos de Goya y sus dibujos preparatorios*, Barcelona, Instituto Amatller de Arte Hispánico, 1949.

SÁNCHEZ CANTÓN, F. J., *The life and works of Goya*, translated by P. Burns, Madrid, Editorial Peninsular, 1964.

VIÑAZA, Conde de la, *Goya, su tiempo, su vida, sus obras*, Madrid, 1887.

YRIARTE, Charles, *Goya*, Paris, Plon, 1867.

ZAPATER Y GÓMEZ, Francisco, *Goya: noticias biográficas*, Saragossa, La Perseverancia, 1868.

Printed in Italy

CONTENTS

---

* Original Spanish.